The Promise of Certainty

Protecting Your Church from the Storms You Don't See Coming

Ron Wadley

COPYRIGHT INFORMATION

ISBN: 9798267835749

Imprint: Independently published

Copyright © 2025 by Ron Wadley

All rights reserved. No part of this publication may be reproduced, distributed, or transmitted in any form or by any means, including photocopying, recording, or other electronic or mechanical methods, without the prior written permission of the publisher, except in the case of brief quotations embodied in critical reviews and certain other non-commercial uses permitted by copyright law.

For permission requests, write to the publisher at:

6777 Camp Bowie Blvd #329
Fort Worth, TX 76116
469.789.0220
info@insurancefortexans.com
www.insurancefortexans.com

Liability Statement

The information contained in this book is provided for general educational and informational purposes only. It is not intended as legal, financial, or insurance advice and should not be relied upon as a substitute for consultation with qualified professionals. All church's circumstances are unique. Readers are encouraged to seek independent counsel to determine appropriate coverage and compliance for their specific situation.

Neither the author nor the publisher assumes any responsibility or liability for any errors, omissions, or outcomes related to the use of this material. Reading this book does not create a client, advisory, or agency relationship with the author or Insurance for Texans.

DEDICATION

*To the pastors, elders, and leaders who carry the weight
of ministry with faith and courage.*

*To the volunteers who show up week after week
to serve with open hands.*

*And to the families who trust the church to be a safe
place for worship, growth, and community.*

This book is for you.

*May it give you clarity, protection, and
the confidence to keep moving the mission forward.*

Table of Contents

COPYRIGHT INFORMATION 2

DEDICATION 3

INTRODUCTION: WHY I WROTE THIS BOOK I

HOW LEADERSHIP, RISK, AND STEWARDSHIP ACTUALLY WORK 1

    PRINCIPLE 1: RISK ISN'T RANDOM MOST OF IT IS PREDICTABLE 2
    PRINCIPLE 2: THERE'S NO EXCUSE FOR DUMB RISK 4
    PRINCIPLE 3: YOU CANNOT BUY PEACE OF MIND AFTER THE FACT 5
    PRINCIPLE 4: GREAT LEADERS START WITH QUESTIONS, NOT ANSWERS 7
    PRINCIPLE 5: BORING IS BEAUTIFUL 9
    LEAD YOUR CONGREGATION & PROTECT YOUR MISSION 11

WHERE YOU ARE NOW, WHERE YOU'RE HEADED, AND WHAT YOU NEED TO GET THERE 13

    WHERE YOU ARE NOW 19
    WHERE YOU'RE HEADED 29
    WHAT YOU NEED 33

HOW TO USE TRUE TEXAS CHURCH INSURANCE'S 3-STEP MODEL 47

ABOUT THE AUTHOR 49

INTRODUCTION:
WHY I WROTE THIS BOOK

I don't know what's worse: a tornado that wrecks your entire building or having to sit through a conversation about tornado insurance. They say insurance is important. They sure don't say it's any fun, though. Most people would rather get a root canal than talk about liability coverage. And trust me, I get it.

But I also know what it's like when the storm hits and you're not ready. That's the moment the insurance conversation stops being boring. That's when the policy in your email inbox potentially becomes the only thing standing between your church and a financial crisis.

You and I both know a book about insurance for churches isn't something people line up to read. So, the fact that you're here tells me something about you. It means you care. It means you're the kind of leader who shows up before the storm hits to make sure you're prepared. In this case, it's with knowledge.

That's why I didn't want this to be another manual collecting dust on a shelf. I wanted the experience of reading this book to matter.

If we're talking about insurance, we're really talking about something bigger. We're talking about leadership. Financial responsibility. Risk awareness. These aren't just policy decisions you make on a whim. They're principles for life.

In my experience, the best leaders and investors all have one thing in common. They know how to manage their emotions. They don't let the highs carry them too far, and they don't ignore the lows. They learn to think clearly in both directions. That's what helps them make good decisions before the pressure cooker turns up.

Most people are familiar with the idea of positive thinking. Norman Vincent Peale wrote a whole book on it. And I believe in that. But I've also learned there's power in the opposite. There's power in negative thinking, too. Not in a cynical way. But in a clear-eyed, sober way. The ability to look at the possible downside and say, "What if this happens?" And then make a plan.

That's what good insurance does. It's not just about policies. It's about the mindset that says, "I'm going to take care of the people and places I've been given to steward." It's financial literacy in action. It's protection with purpose. And it matters.

Because when you lead a church, or a business, or a family, your responsibility goes beyond the day-to-day. You must think about tomorrow. What could go wrong? You must be the kind of person who prepares anyway. That's not fear. That's wisdom. It's leadership.

That's what we do at *Insurance for Texans* everyday with True Texas Church Insurance. We help churches face the unknown with practical tools, clear advice, and The Promise of Certainty.

I grew up as a Baptist preacher's kid. I've been around churches my whole life. I was born in a dusty Panhandle oil field town that had streets made of sand. My family has had a special relationship with Texas churches and the people in them.

I was rocked in the nursery. I've sat in pews on just about every day of the week. And I've sat in deacon meetings to make decisions about a church's present and future. I've felt the weight leaders carry when everything goes sideways. I've seen churches weather fire, flood, lawsuits, and loss. And I've seen what happens when they are covered. Financially, yes. But also, emotionally and spiritually. When the people know, we've got this.

This work of helping churches prepare is holy ground. The ministry doesn't stop when the roof caves in or when a lawsuit comes. The mission keeps going. It must. That's why coverage matters. It protects your ability to gather, to serve, to pray, to preach, to let the Holy Spirit move through a room full of people who aren't sure how it will be fixed but feel safe enough to worship freely.

That's what this is about. Not paperwork. Not policies or terms and conditions that put you to sleep one yawn at a time. It's about protecting your higher purpose. And your peace, too.

A lot of people feel like insurance is a total scam. You pay your premiums every year, hoping you never need to use it. But when something finally happens, that's when the trouble starts. Companies delay, deflect, and deny. They use fine print and legal tricks to avoid paying.

After Hurricane Harvey hit Texas, insurers pointed to flood exclusions to avoid covering storm damage. Harvey made landfall at Port Aransas, then scooted up the Gulf Coast before parking over Houston to drop an immeasurable amount of rain. Entire neighborhoods were underwater. Claims were denied, and people and churches were left hanging wondering what went wrong this time. I think that's infuriating. Honestly, I think it's criminal.

And that's just one kind of storm. One kind of claim. One kind of insurance.

We will cover every threat your church could face and every kind of coverage that counts. From everyday risks to disasters that shut ministries down, you will know what protection you need and why it matters.

If you've ever felt skeptical about how insurance companies operate, you're not alone. And you're not wrong. The system is confusing on purpose. But it doesn't have to stay that way. My job is to walk you through each type of coverage in plain English and explain the phases of church insurance in a way that makes sense.

In 2020, insurers denied about one out of every five medical claims. Cigna was caught using software to automatically reject health claims without a doctor ever reviewing them. One former adjuster even testified before Congress that she was trained to find ways to reduce or deny payouts.

So yes, your skepticism is justified. I feel it too. That's why the agent you work with matters more than the company. Because when disaster hits, you are not calling a boardroom. You are calling a person. And our team knows you, stands by you, and are ready when it counts the most.

At *Insurance for Texans*, we've seen it all. And through it all, we continue to stand on one core belief. Texas churches deserve to be protected by people who understand the mission. That's the heart behind The Promise of Certainty.

Policies are written in legal language. But relationships are built in plain speech. When something goes wrong, you are not calling a lawyer. You are calling your agent. And that person should already be in your corner.

That's why this book exists. Not just to explain coverage, but to help you have clarity before the crisis hits. So, you are not left wondering what's covered or who is going to help. You will already know, because you planned ahead. Making those decisions before the storm hits makes all the difference.

That's the core of what True Texas Church Insurance was created for: Simple clarity, trusted protection, and The Promise of Certainty.

We worked hard to make this book readable and relevant. No jargon. Just real stories and practical tools to help you understand what's at stake and what to do about it before it's too late.

Whether you're a pastor, a deacon, an elder, a volunteer on a committee, or just someone who loves your church, this is for you.

At the end of the day, it's not the tornado or the lawsuit or the premiums that matter. It's protection. Not just for buildings or budgets. But for the heart of your mission. For the sacred rhythm of Sundays. For the ability to gather, to serve, and to worship without disruption.

How Leadership, Risk, and Stewardship Actually Work

Before we get into the different types of coverage, I want to share a few important financial concepts with you. These aren't policy details. You can get those from us directly at ***PromiseOfCertainty.com*** or call the number at the back of the book. Mention this book and my team will walk you through it step by step.

What I want to talk about right now is bigger than that.

Cause' if you understand what I'm about to explain, you'll make smarter decisions than most business owners, let alone church boards. This is where leadership, financial literacy, and stewardship show up.

And I want to be clear. This is something I had to learn the hard way.

I didn't grow up with wealth. I grew up in Lefors, Texas. Tiny town. Baptist preacher for a dad. Hand-me-down clothes. Dirt roads. My parents did their best. And my dad, even when we had almost nothing, always made sure he carried life insurance. My mom used to fight him on it. "We can't afford this." He'd say, "We can't afford not to."

That decision changed everything for our family when he died. It kept my mom afloat for over 20 years. He didn't just take care of us. He gave us time, peace, and space to recover. That's leadership.

I carry that with me in every conversation I have with churches. Because let's be honest… Most of the big disasters people face come down to a lack of preparation, not a lack of faith.

Principle 1:
Risk Isn't Random
Most of it is Predictable

*"The prudent see danger and take refuge,
but the simple keep going and pay the penalty."*
– Proverbs 27:12

People talk about "acts of God" like they are impossible to anticipate. But there's no mystery about where hail hits hardest. We have maps for that. Flood plains are charted. Sexual misconduct risk is tied to access, process, and screening. The problem is not surprise; it is the belief that bad things only happen to *other* people.

Most people think storms in Texas are a spring or early summer thing. The truth is we have a second storm season, especially in the Dallas–Fort Worth area, that hits in the fall. The heat lingers, Gulf moisture rolls in, and the atmosphere turns unstable. Those conditions can light up the sky just as fiercely as any April squall line.

One of the most memorable moments of my career happened on December 26, 2015. The day after Christmas, Dallas–Fort Worth hit ninety degrees. In the middle of winter. That heat mixed with moisture and instability and produced a massive line of storms. Most people will tell you tornadoes do not hit big cities. That night proved them wrong.

An EF4 tornado tore through eastern Dallas. Neighborhoods were wiped out. Entire blocks in Garland disappeared. As agents, we were watching it unfold in real time. Storm chasers were already there because they knew the conditions. This was not random. It was expected. We just did not know how bad it would get.

People died. The financial toll climbed into the hundreds of millions of dollars. Carriers called agents to walk through neighborhoods and confirm which destroyed homes they insured. I called my clients in the area to make sure they were safe. None of them were hurt, but the rebuilding process took a long time. The idea that this storm "came out of nowhere" was a myth. The warning signs were there.

Another example is the weather quirk around Dallas–Fort Worth International Airport. Storms usually move west to east. As they roll in from West Texas, they often explode in size over western Fort Worth. Hail falls. Wind tears things up. But once those storms reach the airport, something happens.

All the jet exhaust, the concrete, and the constant heat from engines create what we called the "heat dome." It sits over the surrounding suburbs and weakens the storms. The hail stops. The winds ease up. The clouds lose their punch. Then, as the system moves past the airport, it reforms and hammers towns farther east. For years we joked the heat dome was undefeated. I would watch huge storms fall apart right in front of my house while the sirens blared, and my family stayed in the safe room.

That changed about eighteen months ago when a storm punched through the heat dome and caused serious damage. Weather is still weather. But it is not random. The patterns are there for anyone paying attention.

We saw the same thing in February 2021 when a polar vortex dropped the entire state below freezing for the first time in a century. The Gulf Coast was in the twenties. Pipes burst everywhere. Power grids failed. The meteorologists warned us for days. People still called it a surprise.

These events prove a point. Nature will always carry some uncertainty, but much of what people call "random" is predictable. The real danger is ignoring what we can see coming. And that is where "No Excuse for Dumb Risk" begins.

Principle 2:
There's No Excuse for Dumb Risk

"To whom much is given, much will be required."
– Luke 12:48

I call it dumb risk because that is exactly what it is. Avoidable. Obvious. Devastating.

Risk exists on a scale. If the forecast calls for rain and you step outside without an umbrella, you get wet. That is minor. Now think bigger. What costs more, a helmet or three years of rehab after a traumatic brain injury? What is easier, buckling a seatbelt or dying in a car crash?

This is not meant to be unkind. It is reality. A car crash is more dangerous than falling off a bike. A bike is more dangerous than getting caught in the rain. Each scenario carries a different level of risk. Each demands a different level of preparation.

And yet, tragedies like Camp Mystic happen.

A girls' summer camp in the Texas Hill Country, built at the meeting point of two rivers. In 2012, the owners asked FEMA to downgrade the flood zone rating for the land. FEMA agreed. Construction continued. Cabins were filled each summer with children just a few feet from the water.

On July 4, 2025, forecasts warned of 10 to 15 inches of rain in less than 24 hours. Flash flooding was a certainty. Many nearby camps evacuated early. Camp Mystic waited too long to act. By the time they moved, roads were submerged. Cabins were filling with water. Counselors were carrying terrified children through chest-high currents.

Lives were lost. Families were shattered. The entire region became a death trap. No insurance policy could ever fully repair what was lost.

All because action came too late. That is dumb risk. Smart leaders kill dumb risk early. This is not fear. This is wisdom. This is love in action.

And let me be clear: my heart breaks for the families who lost their children. It breaks for the counselors and staff who tried to save them. It even breaks for the owners. I do not believe they were careless or malicious. I believe they cared deeply. But care without preparation still leads to tragedy.

This is not about shame. This is about reality. Leadership carries weight. And sometimes, the cost of not looking ahead is more than anyone can bear. Let this be a wake-up call. Then do something about it.

PRINCIPLE 3:
YOU CANNOT BUY PEACE OF MIND AFTER THE FACT

"The wise man built his house on the rock...
the foolish man built his house on sand."
– Matthew 7:24–27

Some lessons hit hard because they are personal. Wayne's story is one of them. Wayne came to me for help with his home and auto insurance. He was frustrated with his old carrier. Getting him covered took almost a month. That was longer than usual. We spent that time digging into what he really needed. I asked questions. I asked a lot of them.

That is when I learned he had two gun safes in his garage. One held family heirlooms. They were firearms more than a hundred years old. They had been passed down through generations. He also had jewelry hidden in another part of the house.

When he first came in, Wayne was focused on price. He did not want to spend more than the year before. Once we talked through the risks, he agreed to pay more for coverage that would protect what mattered.

Three months later, in November, Wayne called me early on a Sunday morning. "I told you I would never make another claim," he said. "But I have a problem."

At two in the morning, his dog started barking and would not stop. He got up to check and saw the house was on fire. He woke his wife. He got her and the dog out. He called the fire department. About forty percent of the house was destroyed.

The fire started in the garage. That was the same place as the gun safes. He had left battery chargers for his power tools plugged in. They sparked and caught the wall. The fire spread through the rest of the house. The heat was so intense that his fully restored 1970s Ford Bronco melted down to nothing. The gun safe held up.

Because we had added proper gun coverage to his policy, every heirloom inside was restored. His total claim ended up at more than two million dollars. The house was rebuilt. His possessions were replaced. He had a place to live during the process.

If Wayne had stayed with his old policy, he would have lost most of it. The house would not have been rebuilt to its original condition. The heirlooms would have been gone forever.

I have seen this same truth outside of insurance. During the 2008 financial collapse, I worked in finance. Billion-dollar companies crumbled overnight. I was there when Lehman Brothers fell. The week before, they took us out for a steak dinner. A week later, they were gone.

I had been watching the markets. I had been preparing. I took my severance and traded conservatively. When I re-entered the workforce three months later, I had more in the bank than the day I was laid off.

The market can stay irrational longer than you can stay solvent. Fires, lawsuits, and economic crashes do not wait for you to get ready. You prepare ahead of time so they do not go as wrong as they could.

For churches, that means you do not want to be figuring out liability limits in the middle of a lawsuit. You do not want to scramble for flood coverage after a hurricane. The time to build your rock foundation is before the storm. Wayne's story proves it. My story proves it. If we are doing our job right for your church, yours never will.

Principle 4:
Great Leaders Start with Questions, Not Answers

"If any of you lacks wisdom, you should ask God…
and it will be given to you."
– James 1:5

Most people operate in triangle mode. They start with very little information. They rush the decision. They end up trapped when the problems get bigger and more complicated.

It is not just that they act fast. They act fast on the wrong criteria. They ask, "What's the premium?" They ask, "What's the deductible?" They think cheaper is better. It feels smart. It feels efficient. But if price is your only filter, you are not making a wise financial decision. You are playing roulette.

The triangle pattern is always the same. Not enough information. Fast choice. Big fallout.

A better model is the funnel. You ask questions up front. You gather more information than you think you need. It feels slower. It is not as clean. But over time, things narrow. Patterns emerge. You get clarity. And more importantly, you get stability.

That is how we work with churches. We ask more questions than most agents. Not because we want to be difficult. Because we have seen what happens when you don't. We have seen churches dropped with no notice because a national carrier decided they were not profitable enough. We have seen ministries forced to sell their land after a flood because the policy they bought did not match the real-world risk they were living in.

A church in East Texas reached out after being non-renewed by their previous carrier. We asked them why. They told us the company was leaving the state. We explained that to put a new policy in place, we needed a loss run. That is a statement from previous insurance carriers showing what claims have been made.

When we received the loss runs, we saw a liability claim against their directors' and officers' insurance. We asked about it. They told us a deacon named "Teddy" had taken money. They said they had removed him from positions of authority. We asked if he was still in the church. They said yes, but he no longer had important responsibilities.

When we said that story to the insurance company, we were hoping would provide coverage, but they refused. They could not understand why Teddy was still part of the congregation. We eventually found the church coverage elsewhere, but it was expensive. They paid more because they had not fully removed the risk.

In another case, a church in San Antonio came to us for help. They took mission trips to Mexico as part of their ministry. They also operated a school in their building during the week.

When we reviewed their policy, we found several problems. They had no coverage for mission trips. They were severely underinsured on property. If a fire happened, they could not rebuild the full facility. They had no coverage for the school.

We showed them the exclusion in their policy that stated there was no coverage for members crossing international borders. They had no idea it was there. They advertised the trips on their website. That meant they could not deny the activity. If anything happened in Mexico, they would face lawsuits and liability without protection.

Most churches focus so hard on price that they miss these gaps. They do not look for the exclusions that open them up to massive loss. In ministry, it only takes one moment for "safe" to turn into "not safe."

The funnel prevents that. It is not paranoia. It is preparation. It is not more complicated. It is more honest. You frontload the complexity so you can lead with peace later.

Good questions create better coverage. Better coverage protects your people. Protecting your people is the point.

PRINCIPLE 5: BORING IS BEAUTIFUL

"Make it your ambition to lead a quiet life… so that your daily life may win the respect of outsiders."
– 1 Thessalonians 4:11–12

Success often looks invisible. It is the disaster that does not bankrupt your church. It is the family that stays because you had coverage to keep programs running. It is the Sunday service that happens without anyone knowing the roof leaked on Friday.

The best policy we sell is the one you never need. That means everything went right. That is not failure. That is victory. Nobody gives you a standing ovation for renewing your property coverage on time. Nobody brings you cookies because you raised your liability limit. But when a crisis hits and your church still stands, that is leadership at work. That is stewardship in action.

You do not need to know everything. But you do need to own your role. Many church leaders dislike dealing with insurance. I understand that. You did not enter ministry to study policy riders or flood maps. But if you serve on the board, or you are responsible for protecting the church, then this is part of your ministry.

When things go wrong, people will look to you for direction. If you froze, fumbled, or ignored warnings, you will live with those choices. Leaders who take this seriously sleep better. They lead better. They protect better. Leaders who do not often wish they had.

Boring is beautiful because when insurance is not the story, you have done your job well. That is good leadership. That is love in action.

My own church in Dallas–Fort Worth offers an example. It is called 121 Community Church. The children's program for birth through kindergarten is called Creation Land. The church organizes the children by age and development. They give them age-appropriate lessons and activities.

I volunteered in Creation Land for years. Every year I went through a background check. I took safety training that covered abuse prevention and explained grooming behavior. The training was repetitive. It was not exciting. But we took it seriously. The goal was to protect children.

Even with those systems in place, a serious incident occurred in a separate church-owned property. The church owns a house where missionaries can stay when they are back in the States. During a routine technology check, they discovered a hidden camera in a bathroom.

They acted immediately. They called the police. They quarantined the device. They limited access to the house during the investigation. They reviewed cell phone data and building access logs. Police arrested an employee.

No one was harmed. The church did not hide the situation. They addressed it openly and accepted the consequences. The systems they had in place allowed them to act quickly and protect others. The work was tedious, but the outcome was far better than it could have been.

The details that feel slow, repetitive, or inconvenient often prevent disaster or reduce damage when it happens. That is why boring is beautiful.

Lead Your Congregation & Protect Your Mission

Let's take a step back for a moment here. What we just covered is not about policy details. It was more about giving you a framework for better leadership. These five principles are the foundation for making more intelligent and informed choices. If you understand those first, you're going to make better choices for your community.

So, let's recap:

- **Risk isn't random.** We have maps. We have data. We know where the danger lives.
- **Dumb risk is deadly.** Trying to save money in the wrong place is how churches go under.
- Peace of mind isn't something you buy in the middle of a crisis. It comes from preparation.
- **Strong leaders ask better questions.** They slow down. They gather context. Then they decide.
- **Boring is beautiful.** When nobody notices the disaster because everything still works, you did your job.

This is stewardship. It's not just spiritual. It's operational. When you lead a church, your decisions carry weight. And the only thing worse than tragedy is knowing you could have prevented it.

As I wrote this summary, I kept coming back to the story of Joseph in Egypt. Pharaoh has a dream. Seven fat cows, seven skinny cows. Joseph interprets it. There's a famine coming, but it won't hit right away. First, there will be seven years of abundance. Most people would've spent wildly during the good times. Joseph doesn't. He stores grain. Builds barns. Gets everything in place. Because he knows what's coming.

And when the famine does hit, Egypt survives. More than that, Israel survives. Families are fed. Nations are saved. And that's not because Joseph was flashy. It was because he was faithful. Because he saw the risk ahead and prepared. That's what leadership looks like.

So, where do we go from here?

You've seen the principles that guide how we protect Texas churches. Now it's time to put them into action with the three-step system we use for every client. It's the roadmap that takes big ideas and turns them into a tailored plan you can put to work. Let's walk through it together.

True Texas Church Insurance delivers the Promise of Certainty through a unique 3-Step System:

WHERE YOU ARE NOW, WHERE YOU'RE HEADED, AND WHAT YOU NEED TO GET THERE

Before we get lost in the details, I want to bring us back to the heart of this whole thing. At *Insurance for Texans*, *The Promise of Certainty* is the result of walking alongside hundreds of churches in our state and refining a simple, proven process for protecting them. One story shows exactly why this is important…

Early in his ministry, Pastor Rick served a small church in the Panhandle east of Amarillo. He and his family loved the community. Sunday mornings were simple and full. Fellowship meals were potluck and heartfelt. The building was not fancy, but there was no debt, and it met their needs. Like most pastors of smaller congregations, Rick wore many hats. He was the preacher, a part-time counselor, a janitor, and the person who looked after the church's insurance. He did not overthink it, but he made sure the church had a policy that covered what mattered.

Then one dark March night, the "just in case" became real.

A tornado tore through the town just after midnight. It lasted only minutes. When the winds stopped, the church was in ruins. Rick lived in the parsonage across the street. Moments before a window shattered across the bedroom, he had carried his young son out of bed.

The windows were gone. The walls and roof were badly damaged. Rain poured in from the storm that followed. His congregation and family were safe, but the building they called home was broken.

Rick did not worry about what would happen next. He had worked with a church insurance advisor to build coverage for events like this. That gave him peace. The peace was not an accident. It was prepared. It was the same kind of peace his faith gave him. Receiving God's grace does not mean we will avoid storms. It means we are not alone when they come and that we have hope on the other side. Insurance works the same way. It does not stop the wind, but it changes how you face the damage.

When the tornado hit, there was no "let's call someone now" moment. Rick could not go back and upgrade his policy. He could not lower his deductible. He could not add flood protection or replacement cost coverage after the fact. It was either done right ahead of time or not at all. Just like grace must be received before our personal day of judgment, insurance must be in place before the day of damage. That is what makes it a certain promise. It is either there when you need it, or it is not. You must act before the catastrophe strikes.

Once the adjuster confirmed how the policy would respond, Rick's focus shifted. He did not get stuck in paperwork or wonder if they could rebuild. He met with church leaders, talked with contractors, and planned where the congregation would gather in the meantime. He led them forward. Good protection lets churches act with purpose instead of fear. It does not replace faith. It strengthens a ministry's ability to keep going after a disaster.

We have seen what happens when churches trust their insurance to national call centers or agents who do not understand your ministries. We have also seen what happens when a storm hits a church that is properly protected with solid coverage. True Texas Church Insurance exists to help churches like yours experience the same peace Rick had. Our job is to make sure your policy matches your actual risks. No fluff. No gimmicks. Just real protection for real churches that want to serve.

Rick would have been the first to say that no policy will ever match the power of God's promise of grace. One is eternal. The other is financial. He loved a good analogy to help people learn. Rick was my dad, and I was the boy he carried from bed that night. He found his promise of certainty many years later when a heart attack caught up with him. I use his teaching style and the lessons I learned from him to lead Insurance for Texans today. Grace gives believers like him and me a foundation that nothing can shake. Insurance, when done right, gives ministries a similar sense of confidence and stability in the face of earthly disasters. That is why getting it right matters. And it will always matter to us. When the wind comes, and it will, you want to lead with clarity, not fear.

Rick's experience is why we start every conversation with the same three questions about your church.

That is our three-part framework: "Where You Are Now. Where You're Headed. And What You Need to Get There."

When all three are aligned, your coverage does more than react to loss. It actively supports your mission.

Every policy we write at *Insurance for Texans* begins here. They're like sunshine, water, and good soil. If you're missing any one of them, nothing's going to take root. But when all three are aligned? That's when your policy works. Let me break that down for you.

Where You Are Now is about geography and current operations. We already know you're in Texas. But where exactly? Because the Panhandle isn't Houston. West Texas has a different story than East Texas. Down by the Gulf? That's a whole different ballgame than up in The Metroplex. Each place comes with its own risks—floods, fires, hail, hurricanes—and your policy must be shaped by those realities. But it's not just the map. Where you are now also includes what you currently have. Meaning, your building, your equipment, your ministries in motion.

Where You're Headed is about vision. What are you wanting to build? Maybe you're a small-town church whose mission is to stay steady and serve the families right in front of you. Maybe you're in a growing city, looking to expand into a second campus, run bigger events, or take your outreach to a new level. Where you're headed is unique to your church. It could be growth. It could be stability. Either way, it matters. Because insurance is not just about where you stand today. It's about protecting the path you're on.

And finally, ***What You Need to Get There.*** This is the piece that pulls it all together. It's the part where we take what's true about your location and your mission and make sure your policy matches it. There's no one-size-fits-all policy. The only thing worse than being uninsured is being misinsured. What you need is coverage that grows with you, coverage that respects your risks, and coverage that doesn't leave blind spots in your ministry.

So, when you hear us talk about *The Promise of Certainty.*, this is what we mean. It's not a catchphrase. It's the outcome of getting this three-part framework right.

And I want you to remember this, whether you use us or choose another agency. These three questions (Where are you now? Where are you headed? What do you need to get there?) will serve you well. Ask them often. Use them to challenge the proposals you get. Use them to weigh your risks and your responsibilities. Build your policy like you build your ministry: intentionally, with wisdom, and with your mission in mind.

Now, once you understand that framework, the rest of this section is going to make a whole lot more sense. Because Texas isn't just one place. It's about five.

You've got the dry, wind-whipped Panhandle up north. Tornado alley. Hail country. Farther west, it turns to desert. Droughts. Wildfires. East Texas is all bayous, trees, and soaking storms. Think mold, flood, and rot. Down south, you're closer to the Gulf. Hurricanes, storm surge, wind damage. Central Texas? That's flash flood central. The Hill Country doesn't look dangerous... until the rain starts falling sideways and the rivers rise fast.

Ask anyone who's been here long enough, and they'll tell you the same thing: you don't pick the weather, but you sure as heck better respect it.

Now stack that up against the second thing. Where's your church's mission headed?

What are you really working toward? A house church in Amarillo doesn't face the same exposures as a multi-campus ministry down in Houston. Your physical location carries weather risk. Your operational vision carries liability. And both of those shape the third piece: What You Need to Get There.

That's what this chapter is here to unpack.

We're going to walk through:

- The five phases of church growth and how risk grows with each step
- How different parts of Texas carry different weather and insurance exposure
- The basic building blocks of coverage: premiums, deductibles, property value, liability layers, and policy design

If you understand these pieces, even at a surface level, you'll be miles ahead of most church boards. You'll be able to ask smarter questions, recognize what matters, and start building a plan that fits your mission... not someone else's template. So, let's start with the different parts of Texas. Because that's where the risk journey begins.

Where You Are Now

Before you can lead your church into the future, you must see clearly where you stand today. Scripture calls us to stewardship that is practical and watchful:

> *"Know well the condition of your flocks and give attention to your herds."*
> *– Proverbs 27:23*

> *"The prudent see danger and take refuge, but the simple keep going and pay the penalty."*
> *– Proverbs 22:3*

God's Word ties wisdom to awareness. Shepherds know every sheep by name and every path their herd travels. Wise leaders recognize danger before it strikes and take steps to protect what has been entrusted to them. This is not fear. It is faith expressed through preparation.

That is why *Where You Are Now* matters. You cannot build a plan for tomorrow if you are blind to the risks that you face today.

Before we can build a policy that works, we need to get clear on where you are now. That comes down to two things: where your church is planted and where your church is in its life cycle.

First, location. Geography shapes your risks. The Panhandle does not worry about hurricanes like the Gulf Coast does. The Hill Country can look bone dry in the morning and be under floodwater by nightfall. And North Texas is its own challenge. The Dallas–Fort Worth Metroplex is a dense stretch of churches, highways, and suburbs where tornadoes, hail, and rising premiums create challenges unlike anywhere else in the state. Fires, floods, hailstorms… Every part of Texas tells its own story, and your policy must respect that.

Second, life cycle. A church renting a school gym on Sundays does not face the same exposures as a multi-site campus with property, payroll, and programs. Growth brings new risks. Stability needs safeguarding. Expansion adds layers you cannot afford to overlook.

Location and life cycle. Those are the two factors that define Where You Are Now. And you cannot build smart coverage until you have a handle on both.

Let's walk through them.

First up: Which Part of Texas is Your Church Located in?

Then we will look at Which Phase of Development is Your Church in Now?

When you know where you are standing and where you are operating, you will know exactly what you need to protect.

WHICH PART OF TEXAS IS YOUR CHURCH LOCATED?

THE PANHANDLE: WHERE HAIL IS A MATTER OF WHEN, NOT IF

The Panhandle is dry and it's flat, too. It's prone to all sorts of extremes. You're going to get wind so strong it'll blow the lawn chairs off your porch... and sometimes even the porch too. Fires roar up real fast and get dangerous, especially when spring winds kick up and there hasn't been any rain for months. In summer, you know that brutal heat. And in winter, it can drop below freezing in just a matter of hours. Hail. That hail... it's not a question of if it's going to start pouring down from the sky. It's more a matter of when. You've already seen it. Roofs getting totaled by hail the size of baseballs or even bigger. Wildfires creeping up on rural sanctuaries. Frozen pipes bursting out of nowhere and flooding entire fellowship halls.

North Texas:
Tornadoes, Hail, and the Metroplex Grind

North Texas isn't the Panhandle. This is the Dallas–Fort Worth Metroplex, a massive stretch of suburbs, highways, and cities running from Dallas through Fort Worth and up to the Red River. The weather here doesn't play around. Tornadoes are a springtime routine, with plenty of EF-0 and EF-1 storms and the occasional EF-4 or EF-5 that takes out neighborhoods, schools, and churches. Hail is another constant. Dallas leads the nation in hail claims, and storms here are strong enough to wreck roofs, smash HVAC units, and punch through stained glass. I've had a customer that had hail the size of a volleyball come through their roof. Flooding might not be the first thing that comes to mind, but older neighborhoods flood fast when drainage systems back up. Even churches far from creeks or rivers can end up with water in the sanctuary. Add in aging buildings with roof leaks, wood rot, and outdated electrical systems, and you've got higher risk and higher premiums. Crime and vandalism also drive costs up, with copper theft, graffiti, and broken windows showing up on more claims. Insurance in North Texas is expensive, and it's getting worse as carriers leave the market or raise deductibles. If your church is in Dallas–Fort Worth, you need to plan, reinforce your buildings, stay on top of inspections, and expect to shop for new coverage every year.

West Texas:
Dry as a Bone, Until it's Up in Smoke

Out west, it's dry as a bone and hotter than a cast-iron skillet left out in the sun. You're not just fighting the heat; you're also fighting drought. Year after year. Water's always scarce, and fires don't take much to get going. The brush is dry, the wind is strong, and before you know it, half the county's up in smoke. Churches out here are spread out, sometimes miles apart, and a fire can tear through before the pastor even hears about it. Roofing's hard to insure. Pipes are old. And when claims do come in, insurers take a long, hard look before they're willing to pay out. A lot of churches get stuck with policies that won't cover enough or come with deductibles that feel like another mortgage.

East Texas:
Where Floods Find You, Whether You're Ready or Not

Now East Texas, that's a whole different story. The Piney Woods are green, humid, and water is everywhere. It rains so much you start to wonder if Noah's going to float by. That red clay doesn't absorb much, so when the rain comes hard (and it often does) it just sits on top and rolls wherever it wants. Churches flood here. Parking lots fill up. Roads wash out. And with all that moisture, mold becomes a serious issue, especially in old sanctuaries without good ventilation. And then you've got the storms. Big ones. Trees fall on buildings. Tornadoes touch down more than folks like to admit. If you're near the Gulf, you can't ignore hurricane season either. Some churches have gone under because they thought their standard policy covered flood. It didn't.

South Texas & The Gulf Coast:
Heat, Hurricanes, and the Floods Nobody Told You About

Way down south, you're looking at heat that never seems to end. Days in the triple digits. Nights that don't cool off. It wears everything out faster. Your roof, your A/C, your people. And just because it's mostly dry doesn't mean you won't see flooding. When a tropical system rolls through, it dumps so much rain, your whole street can go under in an hour. Flash floods hit fast, and the older churches with basements or low-lying sanctuaries are the first to go.

Then there's the coast. Storm surge, high winds, saltwater corrosion. It's not if your building will take a hit. It's when. A lot of churches around here thought they were covered until a hurricane came through and they found out flood was excluded. That's a hard lesson to learn too late.

Central Texas and The Hill Country: Flash Flood Alley— Calm One Minute, Chest-Deep the Next

They call it Flash Flood Alley for a reason. It can be bright and sunny in the morning and a full-blown emergency by dinnertime. The land around here is steep and rocky. Water doesn't soak in. It runs. Fast. Real fast. There've been times where entire church buildings got swallowed up in a matter of minutes. It's heartbreaking. That's what happened at Camp Mystic. And it's not just the floods. The storms hit hard too. Hail, lightning, and winds that'll rip the siding off your building if you're not ready. Churches with big roofs are especially vulnerable. And every summer, the heat creeps higher. We're seeing more 100-degree days every year. Add it all up and Central Texas churches are getting hit from all sides. You're rolling the dice if your policy is not bulletproofed.

Now, you already know where your church is. You know the street. You know the storms. You have patched the roof and prayed through the power outages. You do not need an insurance agent to explain Texas weather to you.

But here is where churches often get blindsided. Insurance companies start with your ZIP code. That is the first filter they use to price your policy. But if that is where the conversation ends, you are at risk of being misinsured.

Two churches in the same ZIP code can have completely different exposures. One might sit on high ground, mostly safe from floods. Another might be a basement-level sanctuary that floods every spring. One might be a hundred-year-old building with an aging roof. Another might have a brand-new metal roof designed to take a beating.

If your insurance provider does not ask the right questions or does not understand the real conditions of your property, you will end up either underinsured or paying for coverage you do not need.

Because no matter where you are, the phase your church is in changes the stakes. A small church renting space does not face the same risks as a multi-campus ministry. Growth brings new exposures. Stability demands protection. Expansion adds complexity. Let's talk about where your church is in its life cycle. Because risk grows as you do.

Which Phase of Development is Your Church in Now?

Where your church is located shapes the kind of storms you face. But where you are in your church's development shapes how exposed you are when they hit. The stage you are in makes a massive difference to your coverage.

A church plant meeting in a living room has a different risk profile than a multi-campus ministry with buildings, programs, and staff. As you grow, so does your exposure. And if your insurance has not grown with you, you are carrying hidden risks whether you realize it or not. The truth is that churches rarely stand still for long. They are either moving forward into new opportunities or settling deeper into established rhythms. Both paths carry risk, and both require intentional planning.

That is why it is not enough to know your address. You also need to know where you stand in the life cycle of your church. Every phase brings new responsibilities, and each one demands a different level of coverage. Let's walk through the five key phases of church development.

Phase 1: The Living Room Church (Startup Phase)

This is how a lot of churches begin. You've got a handful of families, maybe ten folding chairs, a guitar, and some snacks. You're meeting in someone's living room or maybe a backyard. There's no official building, no payroll, and no insurance. And honestly, at this stage, that's fine. You don't have the revenue to justify it, and there's not much to insure. The risk? It's all personal. If something goes sideways, it's on the homeowner.

Phase 2: The Portable Church (Mobile Phase)

Now you are growing. Too many people for the living room. So you are renting space. Maybe it is a school cafeteria. Maybe a recreation center. You show up Sunday morning, haul in the sound system, set up chairs, and pack it all back up when you are done.

Here is the catch. Once you rent space, the landlord will require General Liability Insurance. It is non-negotiable, and it shows up in every lease. That policy is often your first official step into the insurance world. It provides the basic protection you need just to get in the door, but it also sets the stage for more coverage as your ministry grows. We also recommend adding equipment coverage for storage and transport, since your gear is the backbone of your operations. Protecting it means protecting your ability to show up every week and keep the mission moving.

Phase 3: The Seven-Day Church (Permanent Lease)

Now you've leased a full-time space. You're not just popping in on Sundays—you're hosting Bible studies, youth nights, food drives, maybe even hiring your first staff member. At this point, your risk profile changes. You need more than just general liability. You're looking at:

- Pastoral Liability (because not every conflict is spiritual)
- Abuse and Molestation Coverage (if kids are involved, this is critical)
- Directors & Officers (your board members need protection too)
- Workers' Comp (if someone gets hurt on the job)
- Personal Property Insurance (for all the stuff you've accumulated)

It is not overkill. It is maturity. As your ministry expands into a seven-day presence, protecting people, property, and leadership is simply part of growing into the full responsibility of the work God has placed in your hands.

Phase 4: The Property Owner (Ownership Phase)

Now you have bought the building. Or you have built it. Either way, you now have real estate, and with that comes the responsibility of full Property Insurance. But the story does not end there. Property coverage protects the structure, but your ministry is more than bricks and mortar. The way you use the building, the programs you run inside it, and the people who come through the doors all create new layers of risk.

These days, you're probably:

- Accepting online donations → Cyber Liability
- Livestreaming services → Media Liability
- Running big events → Umbrella Liability (for when things really go wrong)

You've got more people coming through your doors. More traffic means more exposure. This isn't just about protecting bricks and mortar—it's about protecting your ministry.

Phase 5: The Mega Church (Large or Multi-Site)

This is where it gets complex. You've got a full campus. Or maybe five. Maybe a school program, daycare, counseling center, and missions sending agency—all under one roof. At this level, you're dealing with:

- Mission Trip Insurance (yes, even for that trip to Guatemala)
- Daycare, food pantry, or coat closet liability
- And depending on your setup, Armed Security Coverage if you've got volunteers packing heat on Sunday morning.

This is where insurance stops being paperwork and becomes risk management at the leadership level. It is not just about terms and conditions. It is about strategy. At this stage, you are not just protecting a building. You are safeguarding a machine that reaches thousands every week.

Summary of "Where Are You Now?"

Before your church can protect what God has helped you build, you as a leader, your board members, and your decision-makers need to get clear on two critical factors.

- Where your church is located
- Where you are in your development journey

These two realities shape the risks you face and determine what kind of coverage is needed.

1. Location Matters

Texas is massive, and no two regions face the same threats:

- **Panhandle:** Hailstorms are routine.
- **North Texas:** The Dallas–Fort Worth Metroplex faces tornadoes, hail, flooding, and some of the highest insurance premiums in the state.
- **West Texas:** Drought and wildfire dominate.
- **East and South Texas:** Floods, hurricanes, and storm damage are common.
- **Central Texas:** Flash floods can appear without warning.

Even two churches in the same ZIP code can face completely different risks based on elevation, construction, and building age. Smart coverage starts with an honest look at your environment, not just your address.

2. Life Cycle Defines Exposure

Churches grow, and growth brings new responsibility and new risk. Liability needs often overlap between phases. Coverage should always reflect your current ministry activity, not just your phase on paper.

Ministry phases and exposures:

- **Startup (The Living Room Church):** Minimal assets, high personal risk.
- **Mobile Phase (The Portable Church):** Renting space requires basic liability coverage.
- **Permanent Lease (The Seven-Day Church):** Increased attendance and programming create greater risk. This stage often calls for pastoral liability, abuse coverage, and workers' compensation.
- **Ownership Phase (The Property Owner):** Owning property introduces additional exposures such as cyber liability, media coverage, and event insurance.
- **Multi-Site (The Mega Church):** At scale, risk management becomes a leadership-level strategy.

Your coverage should always match the real-world risks your church faces today. Failure to align your policies with your ministry's location and life stage can leave you exposed when it matters most.

Where You're Headed

Planning for the future is more than a leadership exercise. It is an act of stewardship and responsibility. When a church looks ahead, it is not only preparing budgets or buildings. It is protecting the people, the mission, and the calling God has entrusted to its care.

> *"Write the vision; make it plain on tablets,*
> *so he may run who reads it."*
> *— Habakkuk 2:2*

> *"Commit your work to the Lord,*
> *and your plans will be established."*
> *— Proverbs 16:3*

God does not call every church to the same path. Some ministries are called to expand, plant new campuses, or launch new outreach programs. Others are called to dig deep where they are, focusing on spiritual growth within a steady congregation. Both paths matter. Both are visions.

Knowing where you are headed means knowing what you are building and who you are serving. It means protecting the mission God has entrusted to you.

You might lead a church that chooses a steady path, like the West Texas pastor who ran the same children's program year after year. The names changed, but the purpose stayed the same. That is a real vision. It is steady and rooted. And it still needs protection.

If your church has a building, you need coverage. If you run programs, you need liability. If you lead people, you carry risk. These truths apply whether you are growing fast or staying the course. The risk does not disappear because you chose a smaller footprint.

Some churches are moving in the other direction. They are expanding what they offer. They might start a second location. They might run a food pantry or daycare. They might launch counseling programs, host large events, partner with nonprofits, send teams on mission trips, or build digital ministries. We have seen how each of these steps changes the risk profile. Adding property changes coverage needs. Hosting public events increases liability. Sending people overseas creates unique exposures.

Every one of these plans comes with risk. Some risks are small. Some are not. But every risk needs to be addressed before it becomes a problem.

Whether your vision is to stay steady or to stretch, the future will not build itself. You will build it. Every decision you make today will either protect it or put it at risk. That is why we are not stopping with where you are right now. We are looking ahead on purpose and designing a plan that fits the ministry you are becoming, not just the one you are leading today.

This is where our Future-Focused Framework comes in. It starts with three questions. On the surface they sound similar. Each one digs into a different layer of your future. Your vision. Your calling. Your stability.

If you lead a team, these questions matter even more. They align your people. They clarify your direction. They move you from fighting fires to building the future. The coverage protects what you build.

QUESTION 1:
FUTURE-BACK VISION.

Step out of the day-to-day for a moment. Picture yourself three years from now. Your church has grown into what you hoped it could be, spiritually, relationally, and operationally. **What happened between now and then that made you feel supported, secure, and fully aligned with your calling?** That is the future we want to plan for. Not just the risks. The wins too.

QUESTION 2:
CALLING AND CLARITY.

Now imagine it is three years from today. You are sitting with your team. The church is thriving. You are reaching the people you were called to serve. You are not putting out fires. You are focused. Equipped. At peace. **What had to be true, organizationally and spiritually, for you to feel that way?** That is what we are building toward. We want to make those things true on purpose.

QUESTION 3:
OPERATIONAL AND LEADERSHIP STABILITY.

Fast forward again. Everything worked. Your systems held. Your team stepped up. The ministries ran strong. When challenges came, you were ready. **What did you build into your leadership, your team, your systems, or your property that gave you that stability?** Did you expand, build, or renovate? Did you improve what you already had? Those choices shape your future risk. That is what your insurance plan should support. Not just protection. Sustainability. Long-term stewardship.

These three questions are simple but powerful. They map out three dimensions of your future. They help us design a plan that does not just react to risk but reinforces your mission. So, let's get clear. Let's get aligned. Let's plan for the church you are becoming.

Up to this point, we have mapped the core realities that determine how your church should be protected.

Where are you now? Your physical location determines the natural hazards you face. Your stage of ministry determines how exposed you are when they hit.

Where are you headed? This could mean staying steady and serving the same families for decades. It could mean launching new campuses, programs, and outreach. Either path carries its own set of risks.

The Future-Focused Framework. Three questions that push you to think beyond the present. See the ministry you want to build. Name the calling you want to protect. Identify the stability you want to sustain.

When you know your location, your phase, and your destination, you can see the gaps. You can decide what needs to be in place to keep your mission from being disrupted.

Now it is time to connect that clarity to the tools that make it real. In the next section, you will see the specific types of coverage that address the actual risks churches face in Texas and beyond. This is a practical reference you can use right away to match your unique situation to a plan that keeps your ministry strong and moving forward, whether you choose to work with us or not.

What You Need

Stewardship means preparing wisely for the future, not just hoping things work out. Jesus taught us to count the cost before we build:

> *"For which of you, desiring to build a tower, does not first sit down and count the cost, whether he has enough to complete it?"*
> *– Luke 14:28*

> *"Through wisdom a house is built, and by understanding it is established."*
> *– Proverbs 24:3*

This section is about building that kind of wisdom into your church's coverage. Knowing where you are gives you clarity. Knowing where you are headed gives you vision. Putting those together shows you exactly what protection your ministry needs to stay safe, stable, and standing.

At the highest level, church insurance has a simple purpose:

- Protect the building and what is inside it.
- Protect the people who lead and serve.
- Protect against unexpected events that could stop your ministry.
- Protect your ability to keep going when things go wrong.

When you plan with wisdom, your church can weather any storm and keep fulfilling its mission.

From there, the details matter. Different types of coverage exist for different risks. Not all of them are obvious until you have lived through the problem they are designed to solve.

Now let's get specific. There are twelve types of coverage every Texas church should consider. The five phases of a church's life cycle are a helpful guide, but coverage needs do not always follow them exactly. Some risks show up early. A church in the Mobile Phase may need abuse coverage if it is already hosting children's programs, even without a permanent location. Always base coverage decisions on current ministry activity, not just phase. I will explain each type of coverage in plain language as if we were sitting across the table. If you have ever looked at your policy and wondered, "Are we actually covered for the stuff that matters?" you are not alone. Most churches do not realize what they are missing until it is too late. Here are the twelve types of insurance coverage every church should seriously consider.

1. Property Insurance: Your Roof Over Ministry

Your building is more than a structure. It is the place where your ministry gathers, serves, and worships. Property insurance protects everything tied to that mission. It covers your sanctuary, classrooms, fellowship hall, signage, technology, furniture, and more. When fire, hail, wind, or vandalism strikes, this coverage helps your church recover quickly.

Premiums across Texas have surged since 2023. Churches with no claims history have seen increases from $12,500 to $73,000 or more. This rise comes from billion-dollar weather events, aging facilities, inflation in construction costs, and stricter underwriting. Insurers now inspect older roofs, building materials, and safety measures more closely. Preparation is essential.

What to check now:

- Confirm your policy pays replacement cost instead of depreciated value.
- Consider adding business personal property coverage to repair or replace the contents that can be damaged during claim scenarios so that you don't have to start over.
- Learn about Tenants Improvements and Betterments is a way to protect any remodeling or finish out work that you have done when you are leasing space.
- Review your wind and hail deductible. Many policies use a percentage of the insured value. For example, 2% of $5 million is $100,000.
- Verify your roof schedule and materials, especially if you have replaced or upgraded your roof recently.
- Add Business Income and Extra Expense coverage to cover the cost of renting temporary worship space and keeping programs running.
- Prepare for inspections and underwriting reviews on buildings over 50 years old to avoid unexpected non-renewals.

Property insurance is the foundation of your protection plan. A well-structured policy gives your church the ability to keep meeting, serving, and rebuilding after a major loss.

2. General Liability:
The Everyday "What If?" Shield

People slip. Kids run around. Cables trip someone during teardown. General liability carries those third-party injury claims and keeps routine accidents from becoming financial shocks. The label sounds broad, but base policies often exclude special events and abuse. Courts also award larger judgments now. Limits of one to two million used to feel fine. Today many churches add an umbrella to reach five million or more.

Tighten the basics:

- Add Additional Insured status for landlords and venues.
- Use written event checklists.
- Require certificates from outside groups that use your building.
- Keep Medical Payments limits practical so you can resolve small incidents quickly.
- If you host festivals, lock-ins, or inflatables, place them under special event coverage or an endorsement before the flyers go out.
- Train greeters and facility volunteers to spot hazards. Fresh eyes prevent claims.

While these steps may seem simple, they go a long way towards preventing claims before they happen.

3. Pastoral Liability: When "You Should Have Done More" Shows Up

Texas pastors carry more than sermons. They counsel, mediate, comfort, and guide. If someone alleges harm from pastoral care, you face professional liability, not general liability. Claims may involve emotional distress, negligence, or failure to refer to licensed help.

Lawsuits tied to counseling and ministry guidance are increasing nationwide, and Texas is no exception. This is not about silencing pastoral care. It is about protecting the pastor and the church so ministry can continue without legal or financial fallout.

What to check now:

- Carry dedicated pastoral or professional liability coverage with at least one million per claim.
- Confirm whether defense costs are inside or outside the policy limit.
- Use a simple intake form for counseling sessions that explains the scope and limitations.
- Set clear referral points for trauma, self-harm, marriage crisis, or abuse cases, directing to licensed professionals when needed.
- Keep factual notes from sessions and store them securely.
- Provide peer review or pastoral supervision so complex cases are shared, not carried alone.

4. Sexual Misconduct / Abuse & Molestation Coverage: Stewardship at Its Most Serious

If your church in Texas works with children, youth, or vulnerable adults, this coverage is essential. It only takes one accusation, true or false, to financially and reputationally devastate your ministry. Many insurers are cutting limits or refusing coverage altogether as claim sizes grow nationwide. Texas ministries face the same challenge, and the stakes are high.

Abuse coverage on standard policies might offer coverage, but it often comes with small limits for an incident. It is important to make sure how defense costs are paid. If your limit is low and defense costs are inside that limit, you could be left high and dry if a judgement is rendered. Seek larger limits with defense costs contained under a separate limit to make sure a bad day doesn't turn into a bad future.

Protection starts long before the policy kicks in:

- Screen every volunteer and staff member with background checks, reference calls, and abuse prevention training.
- Keep two-adult policies for every children's and youth activity.
- Use a documented check in and check out procedure so that kids always get back to whom they belong.
- Document attendance and room assignments.
- Use locked storage for any children's ministry records.
- Educate parents and leaders on grooming behaviors and early warning signs.
- Review your policy exclusions to ensure both defense and indemnity are included for alleged abuse.

A lawsuit here is not just about money. It is about trust. This is why a strong prevention plan paired with comprehensive coverage is one of the most important acts of stewardship a Texas church can take.

5. Directors & Officers (D&O): Protecting the People Who Lead

Many Texas church boards are made up of unpaid volunteers who give their time out of love for the ministry. But if a financial or operational decision goes wrong, their personal assets can be at risk. A building loan dispute in Austin, a budget shortfall in Lubbock, or allegations of mishandled funds in San Antonio can all lead to lawsuits naming individual board members.

D&O coverage defends against claims of mismanagement, breach of fiduciary duty, or failure to follow bylaws. Without it, a board member could face legal costs or judgments personally.

Protect your leaders by:

- Carrying D&O coverage with limits that match the size and complexity of your ministry.
- Set and maintain Audit Practices for bank accounts.
- Review retirement planning programs for fiduciary responsibility standards.
- Keeping thorough board meeting minutes and documenting decision-making processes.
- Providing annual training on fiduciary responsibility and conflict of interest policies.

When leaders know they are protected, they can make bold, wise decisions without the fear that a single vote could cost them their home or savings.

6. CYBER LIABILITY: WHEN THE THREAT IS A MOUSE CLICK AWAY

Churches in Texas have embraced online giving, email newsletters, and cloud-based member databases. That convenience makes ministry easier, but it also opens the door to cybercrime. Hackers do not care if you are a business or a nonprofit. If you collect personal information or process payments, you are on the target list.

Data breach claims are less common than weather damage, but when they happen, the costs climb fast. Regulatory reporting, forensic IT services, legal defense, and credit monitoring can easily reach six figures. Most cyber coverage on standard policies offer small amounts of financial protection which often falls well short of those costs. We highly recommend getting a stand-alone policy with less exclusions and larger limits of coverage.

Protect your church by:

- Using multi-factor authentication on all administrative accounts.
- Training staff and volunteers to spot phishing emails.
- Backing up systems regularly and storing backups offline.
- Have a procedure to verify any account information changes that are requested.
- Reviewing whether your cyber policy covers ransomware, wire transfer fraud, and third-party vendor breaches.
- Checking if your coverage includes crisis communication support to help restore trust in your congregation.

Cyber liability coverage is not just a tech problem—it is a trust safeguard.

7. MEDIA LIABILITY: YOUR WORDS, YOUR STREAM, YOUR RISK

In Texas, more churches are streaming services, posting sermon clips, and running social media campaigns than ever before. That public reach is powerful for ministry, but it also creates legal exposure. A sermon illustration, a blog post, or a Facebook caption can lead to claims of misrepresentation, defamation, or invasion of privacy.

Even a false or petty complaint requires a legal response, and those defense costs can drain a ministry budget. Media liability coverage steps in to handle those costs and any damages if you lose.

Protect your message and your team by:

- Confirming your media coverage includes livestreams, archived recordings, and social media posts.
- Using licensed music, images, and video clips.
- Training staff on copyright and intellectual property basics.

- Avoiding personal identifiers in stories unless you have written consent.
- Reviewing whether your coverage extends to guest speakers and volunteers.

Your words matter. Media liability helps make sure a message meant to bless does not become a legal burden.

8. Special Event Insurance: Fun Until It's Not

Festivals in the park. Trunk-or-treats in the parking lot. Youth lock-ins that run until sunrise. These events create connection and joy, but they also carry risk. Many standard liability policies in Texas exclude special events unless they are specifically endorsed. And most church policies exclude coverage for bounce houses or inflatables altogether.

One accident—a child falling from an inflatable, a food poisoning incident at a chili cook-off, or a trip-and-fall at a vendor booth—can result in expensive claims. A standalone event policy is inexpensive compared to a six-figure settlement.

Keep events safe and covered by:

- Adding special event coverage before you promote or host the activity.
- Requiring vendors to provide proof of insurance.
- If you are renting a bounce house or other inflatable items for an event, requiring the vendor to include you as an additional insured on their policy is a must.
- Documenting safety measures, such as first aid stations and clear walkways.
- Having trained volunteers to monitor higher-risk areas like playgrounds or inflatables.
- Reviewing cancellation coverage if your event depends on ticket sales.

Special events are meant to build community, not legal bills. They are opportunities to bring people together, share joy, and open doors for ministry. But one accident or overlooked detail can turn celebration into crisis. With a little planning and the right coverage in place, your church can host events with confidence, knowing the focus stays where it belongs—on connection, fellowship, and the mission you are called to carry out.

9. Workers' Compensation: Caring for the Caretakers

Technically speaking, workers' compensation insurance is optional in the state of Texas. The state doesn't require you to have it in place like every other state. However, if your Texas church has employees, we don't really think it is optional. Let me explain.

Whether your church has janitors, administrative staff, nursery workers, or musicians, things happen. And when it does, workers' compensation not only covers their medical expenses, lost wages, or other expenses related to the injury, but it also protects your church!

If a claim is made and you have this very important coverage in place, your church cannot be sued beyond the limits of insurance. Not only are these expenses for care not coming out of your church budget, but it also protects you from lawsuit damages. This is something most Texas churches don't understand.

Common claims in churches mirror those in other small organizations:

- A custodian strains their back lifting a heavy table.
- A music director trips over cables during setup.
- A children's ministry worker slips on a freshly mopped floor.

Even these minor injuries can create major disputes without proper coverage. This is why it is so important to protect your church.

Protect your team by:

- Carry workers' comp to reduce liability risk and cover employee medical bills and lost wages.
- Training staff in safe lifting techniques and hazard awareness.
- Keeping walkways clear and workspaces well-lit.
- Encouraging prompt reporting of injuries to start claims quickly.

Workers' compensation is not just a legal choice. It is a practical safeguard and a way to care for the people who care for your congregation.

10. Mission Trip & Travel Coverage: Ministry That Moves

In Texas, ministry often extends beyond your own city limits. Churches do not just gather within four walls; they mobilize. You might send a youth group across the border to Mexico, deploy a relief team to Louisiana after a hurricane, or take leaders to a national conference to sharpen their skills. Each of these trips carries spiritual purpose, but they also carry practical risks. The moment you step off campus, your standard property and liability coverage usually stops, leaving your people and your mission exposed.

That is where mission trip and travel coverage steps in. This coverage follows your people wherever they go, whether across the state or across the ocean. It provides protection for medical emergencies, accidents, or sudden illness far from home. It can also safeguard the mission itself by covering emergency evacuation, lost baggage, or trip interruption. Without it, one unexpected incident can turn a life-changing trip into a financial and logistical crisis. With it, your church can focus on serving rather than scrambling.

Strengthen your outreach by:

- Securing coverage before booking travel.
- Verifying that your policy covers international trips and hazardous activities such as construction or medical clinics.
- Training trip leaders on incident reporting and emergency contacts.
- Keeping copies of passports, insurance cards, and emergency plans in both digital and paper form.
- Partnering with carriers experienced in faith-based travel so your needs are understood.

The mission does not stop at the city limits, and neither should your protection. Whether your team is serving across town, across state lines, or across the world, having the right coverage ensures that ministry continues without disruption wherever God calls you to go.

11. FLOOD INSURANCE: WHEN THE WATER RISES

Most property policies in Texas exclude damage caused by rising water. FEMA defines a flood as water covering two or more acres of normally dry land or affecting two or more properties, often from overflowing rivers, storm surge, or rapid runoff. This definition matters because standard property and windstorm policies never cover these events.

If your church sits near a river, creek, bayou, or low-lying area, flood insurance is essential. One stalled storm can dump enough rain to put an entire block underwater within hours. Texas churches have learned the hard way that a "500-year flood" can happen twice in a decade. Without a flood policy, you may have to rebuild entirely on your own.

Secure your building by:

- Checking FEMA flood maps for your exact location.
- Knowing that standard policies may cover wind-driven rain through a wind-damaged opening but never cover flooding from rising water or storm surge.
- Reviewing your deductible and coverage limits.
- Keeping important equipment and documents off the floor in flood-prone areas.
- Pairing insurance with practical mitigation tools like sump pumps and flood barriers.

Flood insurance protects more than your property. It gives you the ability to keep serving your community when the water recedes.

12. LIFE INSURANCE FOR KEY LEADERS: A FINANCIAL SAFETY NET FOR THE FLOCK

Some Texas ministries revolve around a single senior pastor, founding leader, or major donor whose presence anchors both the vision and the resources of the church. When that person carries so much of the weight, their sudden absence can leave a void that is more than emotional. If a leader passes away unexpectedly, giving patterns can shift overnight. Families who were loyal to that person may step back. Staff morale can dip as people wonder about the future. Critical programs may stall without the steady hand that once guided them. In the middle of grief, the church can also face very real financial strain.

Key person life insurance provides a financial buffer in that fragile season. It buys the church time to grieve without rushing into crisis decisions. It creates stability while the board regroups, hires interim leadership, or reassures the congregation that ministry will continue. It can keep outreach programs funded, staff employed, and operations steady until long-term plans are in place. Instead of scrambling to survive, the church can focus on healing and moving forward with strength.

Safeguard your stability by:

- Identifying which roles are mission-critical and financially central.
- Matching coverage amounts to the potential loss of income or giving.
- Keeping policies updated as the church grows or leadership changes.
- Combining insurance with a leadership succession plan.

Life insurance for key leaders is not about replacing a person. It is about protecting the mission they helped build so it can keep moving forward.

Seeing all 12 types laid out like this is not the finish line. This is the starting point for the right policy. On paper, it's just a list. In the right hands, this is going to be a conversation guide. When you sit down with an agent, this list gives you a way to take control. You're not reacting to whatever they bring up. You're leading with what matters most to your church. You can check your current policy against it, spot the blind spots, and push for the coverage that fits your risks. That's where the value lives.

And that's when the three-part framework really starts working for you. *Where you are now* sets the context. *Where you're headed* keeps you thinking ahead. *What you need to get there* turns those two realities into a plan. When you filter the 12 coverages through that lens, you stop treating insurance like a bill and start using it as a leadership tool.

Who cares about collecting insurance terms and definitions? That's not what we're doing. This is about protecting a mission. The same way a pastor prepares a sermon, or a board plans a budget, you prepare your coverage so your ministry can keep going... no matter what happens. That's *The Promise of Certainty*. It's more than peace of mind. It's knowing you've already made the decisions that keep the doors open, the lights on, and the work of the church moving forward when the storm comes.

How to Use True Texas Church Insurance's 3-Step Model

Most people don't make it through a book on insurance. Especially one written for churches. That tells me you care. You're willing to lead, to prepare, and to take responsibility for the ministry God's entrusted to you.

We didn't put this together just to explain policies. We built it for church leaders like you, in situations just like yours, to make the most intelligent and informed decisions possible. This isn't about learning a set of definitions. You always want to protect your people, programs, and purpose you've been called to steward.

You've seen what happens when it goes wrong. The numbers are sobering: in 2023, Texas was hit by 16 billion-dollar disasters, more than any other state. Hail, hurricanes, floods, wildfires—nearly half of all billion-dollar weather events in the U.S. since 1980 have touched Texas. Churches that once shared coverage are now on their own. Premiums have spiked by six figures for some, forcing painful trade-offs: cutting staff, delaying repairs, scaling back ministry.

But the damage isn't just financial. It's emotional and spiritual. Burnout, broken trust, leadership turnover, congregations shaken to the core. When coverage fails, it's the people who bleed first. And once trust is lost, it spreads fast.

I know this personally. I grew up as a pastor's son. I've seen how fragile stability can be—and how much difference preparation makes. My dad died young, but because he carried life insurance, my mom had more than survival. She had a second chance. That choice shaped the way I see this work. It's not about "maybe." It's about "when."

That's where *The Promise of Certainty* comes in. It's more than a phrase. It's the commitment that when the storm hits, you'll already have made the decisions that keep your doors open, your lights on, and your mission moving forward.

So, here's what to do next:

- Use the three-part framework—Where you are now. Where you're headed. What you need to get there—to filter every conversation with your agent.
- Take the 12 coverage types you've just read about and use them as a checklist, not a suggestion list.
- Press for clarity. Spot the blind spots. Close the gaps.

You don't have to do it alone. We've built free resources, tools, and a friendly, consultative team who understands ministry as well as insurance. We're here to help you use this model to protect your purpose and strengthen your future.

The storms will come. Some you'll see on the radar. Some you won't. The question is, will your ministry still be standing when they pass? Let's make sure the answer is yes. **Visit *PromiseOfCertainty.com*** and let's start the conversation today.

About the Author

Ron Wadley is a native Texan who has spent more than two decades in insurance and financial services. He began his career in the actuarial department of a long-term care insurance carrier in 2000, later expanding into broader financial advising and risk management.

In 2017, Ron founded *Insurance for Texans* with a vision to put people and churches first – not corporations. That vision grew into True Texas Church Insurance and The Promise of Certainty, a framework dedicated to helping ministries prepare for the storms they don't see coming.

Ron's work is deeply personal. The son of a Baptist preacher, he grew up surrounded by Texas churches, pews, and potlucks. He has seen firsthand the weight pastors, elders, and deacons carry when disaster strikes. His passion is helping leaders steward their congregations wisely by protecting what matters most: their mission, their people, and their peace.

When he's not working with church leaders, Ron can be found riding one of his many bikes, cheering on his Baylor Bears, or spending time with his wife and their daughters.

THE PROMISE OF CERTAINTY

TAKE YOUR NEXT STEP:

SCAN OR VISIT:
PROMISEOFCERTAINTY.COM